# WAIT!

## Why You Procrastinate
## &
## What You Can Do About It

# PAUL H. BURTON

# WAIT!
## Why You Procrastinate & What You Can Do About It

Paul H. Burton

971-223-3663

paul@quietspacing.com

Copyright © 2016 by Paul H. Burton

ISBN 978-0-9909855-6-3

Illustrations © Dreamstime.com

All rights reserved. No part of this book may be reproduced or transmitted in any form or by any means, electronic or mechanichal, including photocopying, recording or by any information storage and retrieval system without written permission from the author, except for the inclusion of quotations in a review.

Published by:
Paul H. Burton
www.quietspacing.com

Page layout by Mira Digital Publishing,
Chesterfield, MO 63005

Printed in the United States of America

# DEDICATION

For those who wish to enjoy work
as part of a rewarding life

# About Paul H. Burton

Paul H. Burton is a former attorney, software executive, and successful entrepreneur. He helps clients gain command of their days, get more done, and enjoy greater personal and professional satisfaction. Paul is available for keynote presentations, interactive seminars, and individualized coaching services. You can learn more about Paul and his work at www.quietspacing.com.

## Other Books by Paul H. Burton
— Available on Amazon

- *Done!: Time Management Strategies for Regaining Command of Your Day*

- *Done . . . Again: Ten New Ways to Make Better Use of Your Time*

- *Triage: Rescuing Your Inbox*

- *Send: A Dozen Ways to Make Email Productive Again*

- *Orchestrate: Four Productivity Skills Every Manager Needs*

- *The Waterfall Effect: Six Principles for Productive Leadership*

# CONTENTS

# The Path From Waiting Less
# To Doing More

E veryone procrastinates. It's a natural behavior. The question is whether our procrastination has negative consequences. If so, how often? The more often procrastination negatively affects our work, the more it's negatively affecting our lives.

Moreover, procrastination is a behavior pattern, not a job responsibility. So, if we're procrastinating at work, we're likely procrastinating at home. Again, it's only the procrastination that generates negative consequences that matters. However, there are only rare occasions where procrastination produces a positive result. Consequently, it's fair to state that procrastination is not a good thing.

Another way to look at this issue is to consider the benefits from procrastinating less. First, we'd be more responsive—we'd get back to clients and colleagues sooner with actual work product. And, speaking of work product, if we waste less time procrastinating, we'll spend more time producing work—good quality work—because we have more time to do it. Finally, we'll reduce our risk of making mistakes if we're not rushing all the time due to our own self-destructive procrastination. It just makes sense that spending more time doing productive work has a positive impact on our clients and our careers.

This book focuses on why we procrastinate and what we can do about it. It's structured as a set of multiple-choice questions. The answers to each question are explained on the following page. The idea is to make it fun to learn more about procrastination, why we do it, and how we can do it less often.

- **Part I: Fun Facts.** This section covers a host of fun facts about procrastination. It also measures your self-assessed level of putting things off.

- **Part II: Education.** This section explores why—scientifically—we procrastinate. It's loaded with interesting information on how we humans engage with the things that must get done.

- **Part III: Techniques.** The section focuses on how we can productively manage procrastination. Not every tip or trick will work for everyone. However, finding one or two new techniques for overcoming procrastination makes this section valuable.

Let's see what we can learn about procrastination and how to minimize the negative effects it can have on our wellbeing. Turn to the next page to get started.

# Interesting Things About Procrastination

This segment covers random facts about procrastination that will make you smile as well as think. Work through the questions and answer them as best as you can. The answer to each is on the reverse page. Also, there is a scoring grid at the end of the section to assist you with tracking the information covered.

# Fun Facts Question #1

**Do you procrastinate?**

O **Yes**

O **No**

# Fun Facts Answer #1

If you answered yes, you're in the right place. Continue on to learn a few fun facts about procrastination. Later, we'll explore why we procrastinate and what we can do to minimize procrastination's negative consequences.

If you answered no, go do something more productive! But, before you go, you might want to continue on to learn about pre-crastinators and how overachievers suffer from different, but equally significant, productivity problems.

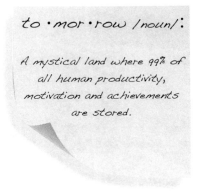

to · mor · row /noun/:

A mystical land where 99% of all human productivity, motivation and achievements are stored.

# Fun Facts Question #2

## What percentage of the population do you think procrastinates?

O 35%

O 55%

O 75%

O 95%

# Fun Facts Answer #2

95%. That's what Piers Steel of the University of Calgary estimated after spending a decade studying procrastination. In his book *The Procrastination Equation: How to Stop Putting Things Off and Start Getting Stuff Done,* Professor Steel states that procrastination stems from three factors: first, a lack of confidence; second, disinterest in the task; and third, impulsive behaviors, which lead us away from the work at hand and toward unproductive activities. We'll explore various explanations for procrastination further in Part II: Education, as well as techniques of combatting it in Part III: Techniques.

# Fun Facts Question #3

**How would you categorize your level of procrastination, assuming that you are part of the 95% of the population who procrastinates?**

O Minimal

O Moderate

O Significant

O Chronic

# Fun Facts Answer #3

It's interesting to note that Professor Steel, author of *The Procrastination Equation,* found that 25% of us are **chronic** procrastinators. Regardless of how you rated yourself, Part III: Techniques will help you minimize that behavior and get more done.

# Fun Facts Question #4

**Procrastination can facilitate
what aspect of work?**

O **Routine tasks**

O **Creative tasks**

O **Organizational tasks**

O **Complex Tasks**

# Fun Facts Answer #4

Creative tasks. Adam Grant, author of *Originals: How Non-Conformists Move the World*, cites research that found that ideation—generating new ideas (being creative)—was enhanced when people were instructed to wait until closer to the deadline to start working.

This analysis was based on a study of two groups of students who were asked to write business plans. The first group was instructed to start immediately. The second group was advised to wait before starting their work. The procrastinators' plans were rated 28% more creative by an independent review panel.

Note the trap for the unwary here. This result was *only* true of tasks requiring new ideas to be created. Non-creative tasks largely do not benefit from procrastination.

# Fun Facts Question #5

**According to *Originals* author Adam Grant, the opposite of a procrastinator is a what?**

O Type A personality

O Pre-crastinator

O Non-conformist

O Lazy bum

# Fun Facts Answer #5

Pre-crastinator. Grant pokes fun at himself during an interview about his book by saying that he tends to place too much focus on getting things done *in advance!*

Interestingly, overachieving comes with its own baggage. Stress is stress, and it has negative mental and physical consequences. We'll explore those consequences below, along with remedies for a healthier and happier life.

# Fun Facts Question #6

**Fallingwater, Frank Lloyd Wright's architectural masterpiece, was reportedly sketched how long before a client meeting?**

O **30 seconds**

O **30 minutes**

O **30 hours**

O **30 weeks**

# Fun Facts Answer #6

30 minutes. This fun fact was cited by Stephanie Vozza in her Fast Company article titled "How the Most Productive People Procrastinate," October 14, 2015. See the article at http://www. fastcompany.com/3052041/secrets-of-the-most-productive-people/ how-the-most-productive-people-procrastinate.

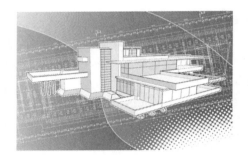

# Fun Facts Question #7

**People who were shown pictures of themselves aged several years were more likely to do what?**

O **Get cosmetic surgery**

O **Lose weight**

O **Increase retirement savings**

O **Run from the room screaming**

# Fun Facts Answer #7

Increase retirement savings. Hal Hershfield, a psychologist at UCLA Anderson School of Management, conducted a study where he asked subjects what they would do with $1,000. Those who were first shown a digitally aged version of themselves chose to invest *twice* as much into retirement as those who did not see the enhanced picture. Bank of America, Merrill Lynch, and Allianz are offering clients a web service that "ages" a current photo of their customers with the hope that it will prompt them to increase their retirement savings.

# Fun Facts Question #8

**Brian Tracy, the famous motivational speaker, recommends we do what with "That Frog?"**

O **Boil it**

O **Watch it**

O **Eat it**

O **Train it**

# Fun Facts Answer #8

Eat it. In one of his most successful books, *Eat That Frog,* Tracy recommends that we tackle the hardest task on our list first each day. That's when we have the most energy and are the most focused.

# Fun Facts Question #9

**Which of these two activity-based characteristics matches your procrastination behaviors?**

O **Rest-seeking**

O **Fun-seeking**

# Fun Facts Answer #9

Rest-seeking procrastinators would rather not exert themselves at all. Fun-seeking procrastinators enjoy being busy but would rather be active doing things that they enjoy. So, to answer this question, we have to ask ourselves, "What type of alternative activity do we seek out when we're procrastinating—a low-energy one or a high-energy one?"

# Fun Facts Question #10

**A counter-intuitive procrastination hack is to which of the following?**

O Drink coffee

O Indulge your procrastination

O Make a meal

O All of the above

# Fun Facts Answer #10

All of the above. One way to trick ourselves into working more now is to make a deal with our procrastinating selves. Instead of saying "no" to doing something non-productive, say "not right now." Make an agreement with yourself to get a certain amount of work done, then go for a cup of coffee or make a meal. "No" is a much harder battle to fight than "later."

Another terrific way to continually get things done is to employ the Pomodoro Technique. Francesco Cirillo invented the Pomodoro Technique in the 1980s. The concept behind this proven system is to think about time in small increments instead of long intervals. Focusing effort into short bursts of time—twenty-five minutes is the preferred length—increases our ability to get things done. A five-minute break is recommended after each interval until four intervals have been completed. Then, a longer break—fifteen to twenty minutes—is recommended. This technique treats the brain like a sprinter as opposed to a marathoner. Part II: Education teaches us that modern brain science supports this sprinter concept.

# Part I: Fun Facts – Scoring Grid

Below is a quick review of the questions and answers in one table.

| Question # | Question | Answer |
|---|---|---|
| 1 | Do you procrastinate? | Self-assessment |
| 2 | What percentage of the global population do you think procrastinates? | 95% |
| 3 | How would you categorize your level of procrastination, assuming that you are part of the 95% of the population who procrastinates? | Self-assessment |
| 4 | Procrastination can facilitate what aspect of work? | Creative tasks |
| 5 | According to *Originals* author Adam Grant, the opposite of a procrastinator is a what? | Pre-crastinator |
| 6 | Fallingwater, Frank Lloyd Wright's architectural masterpiece, was reportedly sketched how long before a client meeting? | 30 minutes |
| 7 | People who were shown pictures of themselves aged several years were more likely to do what? | Increase retirement savings |
| 8 | Brian Tracy, the famous motivational speaker, recommends we do what with "That Frog?" | Eat it |
| 9 | Which of these two activity-based characteristics matches your procrastination behaviors? | Self-assessment |
| 10 | A counter-intuitive procrastination hack is to which of the following? | All of the above |

# Part I: Fun Facts—Conclusion

The first section's over! Was it interesting? Did you learn something new?

The hope is that this format is engaging and fosters an interactive learning environment. Gaining insight into how prevalent procrastination is offers us some relief. It's also interesting to see how much work is being done to understand and help people minimize unproductive behaviors so they can lead more rewarding lives.

Let's see what the next section—Part II: Education—can teach us about why we procrastinate.

# Why You Procrastinate

Brain science has advanced so quickly over the last few years. The information gleaned from biochemistry and neurology have offered many new insights into why we procrastinate. Work through the questions below and take a peek into the wealth of knowledge we've learned so far.

Again, the answers appear on the reverse page and there's a scoring grid at the end of the section to assist you with tracking the information covered.

# Education Question #1

**Why do you procrastinate?**

O I work best under pressure

O My life has gotten so busy

O I'm not good at managing my time

O I want things done perfectly

# Education Answer #1

Every answer listed is an excuse, not a reason.

- No one works best under pressure; it becomes a habit because we procrastinate.

- Our lives haven't gotten busier; we've continued to mature naturally.

- Time can't be managed; only behaviors can be managed. Perfectionism is a false god on many levels.

- Nothing is ever truly perfect, and attempts to achieve perfection only waste the time we have to deliver excellence.

# Education Question #2

**Which of these is *not* a consequence of procrastination?**

O Feeling bad about ourselves

O Losing the respect of others

O Failing to achieve success

O None of the above

# Education Answer #2

None of the above. Putting things off comes with a heavy toll. Finding ways to feel fulfilled and rewarded is getting harder in the frenetic always-on modern world. Procrastination delivers a small amount of immediate relief but does so at the cost of lost actualization.

# Education Question #3

**A 2015 study found that procrastinators are more vulnerable to what health risk?**

O **Hair loss**

O **Diabetes**

O **Hypertension/cardiovascular disease**

O **Diverticulitis**

# Education Answer #3

Hypertension/cardiovascular disease. Fuschia Sirois authored the results of a study in the *Journal of Behavioral Medicine* that found a positive correlation between procrastination and hypertension and cardiovascular disease. The study was published in June 2015 and can be found at http://nymag.com/scienceofus/2015/03/procrastination-is-not-great-for-your-heart.html.

# Education Question #4

**Chronic procrastination is more pervasive than which of these health issues?**

O **Heart disease**

O **Depression**

O **Kidney failure**

O **Plantar fasciitis**

# Education Answer #4

Depression. Dr. Joseph Ferrari, professor at DePaul University and author of *Procrastinating: The No Regrets Guide to Getting It Done* reported that about twenty percent of the US adult population are chronic procrastinators. That percentage is higher than the percentage of people suffering from phobias and depression!

# Education Question #5

**Why does surfing the Internet release dopamine into the brain?**

O We all secretly love cats

O Our brains are wired to reward novelty

O Surfing anything is cool and fun

O Engaging in complex tasks is rewarding

# Education Answer #5

Our brains are wired to reward novelty. Reward is an important aspect of how our brains work. For example, we tend to delay things that don't offer an immediate reward. That's why laborious or involved tasks tend to be those that we procrastinate. Immediate reward activities—like surfing the web—hold a strong influence over what we want to and what we will do next. That's why social media is such an attractive nuisance.

# Education Question #6

**Procrastination pits the prefrontal cortex against which other part of the brain?**

○ **Cerebellum**

○ **Limbic system**

○ **Cerebrum**

○ **Cartoon characters**

# Education Answer #6

Limbic system. Neuroscientist Paul MacLean developed the triune brain theory in the 90s. His theory separates the brain into three separate but interrelated parts: the reptilian brain, the limbic brain, and the neocortex.

- The reptilian brain controls our vital functions—heart rate, breathing, etc.

- The limbic brain is our emotional center.

- The neocortex is where logic resides.

Procrastination is triggered by fear—an emotion residing in the limbic area. Fear is the most powerful of all emotions and has historically ensured our survival. Using logic, the neocortex struggles to overcome the "fear" of failure, so we procrastinate.

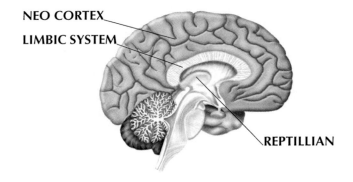

NEO CORTEX

LIMBIC SYSTEM

REPTILLIAN

# Education Question #7

**The majority of people are most productive during which part of the day?**

O Mid-morning

O Mid-day

O Mid-afternoon

O Mid-evening

# Education Answer #7

Mid-morning. In 2012, The Wall Street Journal identified mid-morning as the best time of the day to do complex cognitive work. This gives credence to Brian Tracy's frog-eating theory. There are some other interesting facts in the WSJ article titled "The Peak Time for Everything," which can be viewed at http://www.wsj.com/articles/SB10000872396390444180004578018294057070544.

# Education Question #8

Email is a disguised procrastination strategy because it's easier to consume information than it is to do which of these?

O Do the work

O Create information

O Stay focused

O Ask for help

# Education Answer #8

Create information. It takes much more mental energy to create information—do the work—than it does to consume information. Reading emails and crafting short responses are similar to other forms of media consumption—passive and low energy. Beware the snake in the grass that is "being responsive" via email.

# Education Question #9

**What was the Russian psychologist Bluma Zeigarnik doing when she noticed the effect that carries her name?**

O Dining in a restaurant

O Experimenting in her lab

O The laundry

O Walking her dog

# Education Answer #9

Dining in a restaurant. The Zeigarnik effect states that unfinished tasks are more likely to get stuck in your memory, and thereby get done, than tasks that are not yet started. Bluma Zeigarnik was dining in a restaurant when she first noticed that waiters only remembered orders that were in the process of being served. Once the orders had been served, the waiters forgot the details of the orders entirely. She confirmed her hunch in subsequent lab studies.

# Education Question #10

**Greek philosophers called acting against our better judgement Akrasia; what's the modern explanation?**

O **Laziness**

O **Time inconsistency**

O **Completion complex**

O **Avoidance disorder**

# Education Answer #10

Time inconsistency. The human brain tends to value immediate rewards more highly than future rewards. Whenever we make *plans,* we're making plans for our future selves. However, when we make *decisions,* we are doing so for our present selves. If there's a conflict between the needs of our future selves and those of our present selves, the present self generally wins—instant gratification. That's why the ability to delay gratification is such a great predictor of success in life.

Consider the story of Victor Hugo and his difficulty writing *The Hunchback of Notre Dame.* He continually put off his publisher, promising him that the book was almost finished. This went on for over a year until his publisher finally set a deadline six months away.

Hugo devised a strategy where he sent all his clothes away save one large shawl. This left him with nothing he could wear outside. Extreme as it was, the strategy worked. He finished his book by his publisher's deadline. We'll explore less extreme methods for minimizing procrastination next, in Part III: Techniques.

## Victor Hugo

# Part II: Education—Scoring Grid

Below is a quick review of the questions and answers in one table.

| Question # | Question | Answer |
|:---:|:---|:---|
| 1 | Why do you procrastinate? | Self-assessment |
| 2 | Which of these is *not* a consequence of procrastination? | None of the above |
| 3 | A 2015 study found that procrastinators are more vulnerable to what health risk? | Hypertension/ cardiovascular disease |
| 4 | Chronic procrastination is more pervasive than which of these health issues? | Depression |
| 5 | Why does surfing the Internet releases dopamine into the brain? | Our brains are wired to reward novelty |
| 6 | Procrastination pits the prefrontal cortex against which part of the brain? | Limbic system |
| 7 | The majority of people are most productive in during which part of the day? | Mid-morning |
| 8 | Email is a disguised procrastination strategy because it's easier to consume information than it is to do which of these? | Create information |
| 9 | What was the Russian psychologist Bluma Zeigarnik doing when she noticed the effect that carries her name? | Dining in a restaurant |
| 10 | Greek philosophers called acting against our better judgement Akrasia; what's the modern explanation? | Time inconsistency |

# Part II: Education—Conclusion

The more we learn about how we think, the more interesting things get. Who would've guessed that procrastination is the result of instinctual survival mechanisms? And, what about the idea that endorphins—the feel-good hormones—indirectly promote putting things off!

Let's turn to Part III: Techniques to see what we can do to reduce how much we procrastinate so we can feel more accomplished.

# What You Can Do About It

We are armed with the knowledge that procrastination isn't a weakness of mind. A series of complex mental and physical forces are at play. It's no surprise that successfully dealing with procrastination is no simple matter. Work through these questions to find some techniques to help you minimize the amount of procrastination you experience daily. The answers are on the reverse page and a scoring grid is at the end of the section.

# Techniques Question #1

**Exercising at midday can add how much productivity to your day?**

O 7%

O 17%

O 30%

O 75%

# Techniques Answer #1

17. The British newspaper, *The Guardian,* reported some very interesting results of a study conducted by Jim McKenna at Leeds Metropolitan University. McKenna's team studied 200 people who regularly engaged in thirty to sixty minutes of exercise during their lunch period. The study group demonstrated a seventeen percent increase in their performance over those who did not exercise. That's the equivalent of ***doing eight hours of work in seven.***

# Techniques Question #2

**What alternative practice has demonstrated positive results around procrastination?**

O Meditation

O Self-compassion

O Playing a "power song"

O All of the above

# Techniques Answer #2

All of the above.

- Meditation slows our physical and mental processes down and gives us perspective on what needs doing when.

- Research has demonstrated that the more we can forgive ourselves for past procrastination, the more likely we are to take action now.

- Playing music that energizes us puts us in a positive frame of mind and increases the actions we'll take.

# Techniques Question #3

**Which of these suggestions are actual procrastination fighters?**

O **Pander to the limbic system**

O **Be more disciplined**

O **Commit everything to a list**

O **Eat Oreos**

# Techniques Answer #3

Pander to the limbic system. As discussed in Part II: Education, the limbic system is wired to reward short-term benefits over long-term ones. Using this natural predisposition to fight putting things off requires us to eliminate unpleasantness associated with doing a task. Have to read a lot of paperwork? Do it in your favorite chair—at the office or at home. The point is to piggyback the pleasant with the less desirable to trick the limbic system into helping us get the work done.

**WAIT!** Why You Procrastinate & What You Can Do About It

# Techniques Question #4

**How long does it take to overcome procrastination on a specific project?**

O Five minutes

O Ten minutes

O Fifteen minutes

O Twenty minutes

# Techniques Answer #4

Five minutes. In another application of the Zeigarnik effect, research has demonstrated that committing to just five minutes of effort is enough to get deeply involved in the task. Once we've "opened" that task, we're likely to finish it!

**WAIT!** Why You Procrastinate & What You Can Do About It

# Techniques Question #5

Rory Vaden, author of *Procrastinate on Purpose,* recommends that we use what to get the *right* things done?

O Pen and paper

O Productivity coach

O Matrix analysis

O Focus funnel

# Techniques Answer #5

Focus funnel. Vaden suggests that it's important to understand the distinction between important, urgent, and significant.

- Important is how much it matters.

- Urgent is how soon it matters.

- Significant is how long it matters.

We often fall prey to the sense of urgency tied to everything we receive. Functionally, we respond to the latest and loudest, often leaving the most important and most significant behind. Stop, take a moment to run items through the focus funnel, and then get started on what now seems to be the best use of the available time.

# Techniques Question #6

**Which of these questions is most effective in overcoming procrastination?**

○ What one thing can I do to get started?

○ What are my three biggest priorities today?

○ What will go wrong if I don't do this now?

○ All of the above.

# Techniques Answer #6

All of the above. These questions are different, but they all focus on the same thing—motivation.

- The first question reduces the effort to one action, which is less daunting than a whole project.

- The second question joins the human mind's preference for "3s" with prioritization, which can motivate us to action. Chris Bailey spent a year testing various productivity hacks. In his book *The Productivity Project*, he found that writing down three significant tasks to get done by day's end increased the likelihood of those things getting done.

- The last question focuses on the negative consequences of *not* doing the task, which can be equally motivating.

# Techniques Question #7

**Which of these is *not* a technique for managing procrastination?**

O Clear clutter where you can

O Disable unnecessary distractions

O Play a video game

O Pursue excellence rather than perfection

# Techniques Answer #7

Play a video game. Video gaming is the fun-seeking procrastinator's lair. Video games aren't inherently bad, but they are often the distractions of choice. Here's an explanation for why the other suggestions work:

- Clear clutter where you can. A quiet physical space promotes a quiet mental space, which allows for greater focus and productivity.

- Disable unnecessary distractions. Turning off interrupting technology allows for better focus. Turn it back on when the work is done.

- Stop being a perfectionist. Excellence is a very high standard. Striving for perfection in a time-compressed working environment only delays delivering excellence.

# Techniques Question #8

**What's the best way to bounce back from a lost day?**

O Taking a coffee break and relaxing

O Creating a list for the next day

O Coming in early the next day

O Staying later that night

# Techniques Answer #8

Creating a list for tomorrow. Some days just get away from us. The emergencies pile up, and we spend our whole day reacting to what comes at us. One effective way to deal with a discouraging day is to make a *small* to-do list for the next day. This does two things. First, it raises our spirits to see what important things we will get done the next day. Second, the act of doing creates more energy to get more done. It's a positive feedback loop. So, the next time the day turns disastrous, focus a little energy on the next day to help regain a productive momentum.

# Techniques Question #9

**Which of these is another good way to get a handle on what needs doing?**

○ Putting everything in a visitor's chair

○ Working until everything's done

○ Using a prioritization mechanism

○ Giving it all to someone else

# Techniques Answer #9

Using a prioritization mechanism. We live in a complex and fluid world. Finding ways to simplify things makes them more attainable. One idea is to label things as 1st Order Priority, 2nd Order Priority and 3rd Order Priority. Another is to mark them with a red highlighter for stopped, a yellow highlighter for percolating, and a green highlighter for needs doing. Work styles vary, but reducing tasks to three or four simple categories splits the entirety into more manageable segments.

Mike Vardy, CEO of Productivityist, has another take on this concept. He assigns "modes" to each task. That way, he can align his work efforts with whatever mode he is in. Modes can be very broad: Resource Mode (Outlook or Word), Family Mode (when he's with the family), or Energy Mode(s) (high, quiet, early).

# Techniques Question #10

**Which of these strategies do you like for fighting procrastination?**

O Use a commitment device—a strategy to improve behavior by increasing obstacles to or costs of bad behaviors.

O Reduce the friction of starting—ritualize when certain things get done to create a habit.

O Utilize implementation intentions—determine exactly when and where something will happen to lock it into the mind

# Techniques Answer #10

Self-assessment.

- A commitment device increases the difficulty of engaging in a bad behavior. For example, remove Facebook from the phone and only allow it on the tablet, which stays at home.

- Ritualizing behavior reduces the friction of starting by forming a habit. Finalize timesheets by the end of each day. After a while, it becomes a habit and can demark the end of the working day.

- Implementation intentions focus our intent on a specific date/time/place for a specific activity. The vagaries are eliminated, increasing the likelihood of action.

# Part III: Techniques—Scoring Grid

Below is a quick review of the questions and answers in one table.

| Question # | Question | Answer |
|:---:|:---|:---|
| 1 | Exercising at midday can add how much productivity to your day? | 17% |
| 2 | What alternative practice has demonstrated positive results around procrastination? | All of the above |
| 3 | Which of these suggestions are actual procrastination fighters? | Pander to the limbic system |
| 4 | How long does it take to overcome procrastination on a specific project? | Five minutes |
| 5 | Rory Vaden, author of *Procrastinate on Purpose*, recommends that we use what to get the **right** things done? | Focus funnel |
| 6 | Which of these questions is most effective in overcoming procrastination? | All of the above |
| 7 | Which of these is *not* a technique for managing procrastination? | Playing a video game |
| 8 | What's the best way to bounce back from a lost day? | Create a list for the next day |
| 9 | Which of these is another good way to get a handle on what needs doing? | Using a prioritization mechanism |
| 10 | Which of these strategies do you like for fighting procrastination? | Self-assessment |

# Part III: Techniques – Conclusion

There are as many ways to combat procrastination as there are to engage in it! Take one or two suggestions from this segment of the program with you to minimize the negative consequences that procrastination inflicts on us when we let it happen.

—Conclusion—

# Making The Most Of The Time You Have

Wow! Who would've thought that there was so much to learn about procrastination? It was a quick and engaging trip into the ubiquitous world of putting things off. We all do it to some degree; there are lots of reasons why and just as many ways to overcome it to get on with the work.

Did you learn something interesting in the program? Can you implement one or more of the techniques to beat the procrastination trap? Are you done waiting and ready to starting doing more?

Let's get to it so we can enjoy productive and satisfying careers.

—Bibliography—

# More Resources
# For Combating Procrastination

Procrastination is a popular field of study, and much is being written about it. Here are citations to the works referenced above, as well as some additional resources to explore.

**Books**

*The Procrastination Equation: How to Stop Putting Things Off and Start Getting Stuff Done*, Piers Steel, HarperCollins, 2010.

*Originals: How Non-Conformists Move the World*, Adam Grant, Penguin Group, 2016.

*Eat That Frog: 21 Great Ways to Stop Procrastinating and Get More Done in Less Time*, Brian Tracy, Berrett-Koehler Publishers, 2nd edition, 2006.

*Procrastination: The No Regrets Guide to Getting It Done*, Dr. Joseph Ferrari, Wiley, 2010.

*The Productivity Project: Accomplishing More by Managing Your Time, Attention, and Energy*, Chris Bailey, Crown Business, 2016.

*Procrastinate on Purpose: 5 Permissions to Multiply Your Time*, Rory Vaden, Penguin Group, 2015.

## Online Self-Assessment

Dr. Linda Sapadin created an online self-assessment to determine what type of procrastinator you are. Her research is exhaustive and too broad for the scope of this program. However, if you're interested in learning more about her work, and yourself, you can take her free online procrastination self-assessment at http://userpages. umbc.edu/~koconne1/605TheAdultLearner/pquiz1.htm.